Living Parables

Illustrating
The Message
With Drama

Timothy W. Ayers

CSS Publishing Company, Inc., Lima, Ohio

LIVING PARABLES

Copyright © 1998 by
CSS Publishing Company, Inc.
Lima, Ohio

Library of Congress Cataloging-in-Publication Data

Ayers, T. W. (Timothy Wayne), 1950 -
    Living parables : illustrating the message with drama / Timothy Ayers.
        p.   cm.
    ISBN 0-7880-1171-5 (pbk.)
    1. Drama in public worship. 2. Drama in Christian education. 3. Christian drama,
American.   I. Title.
BV289.A84 1998
246'.72—dc21   97-29589
                                                                          CIP

ISBN: 0-7880-1171-5   PRINTED IN U.S.A.

Living Parables is an outgrowth of many years in the ministry and my association with some truly great Christian people. I've worked with wonderful ministry partners like Jack Nelson (remember the "Single Cell Amoeba" drama, Jack), Tom Lewellen, Steve Christensen, Tracey Pitts, Mark and Linda Siersma, Dick Loizeaux, John Cross, Clyde Glass, Dr. Chuck (Sailor Sam) Christiansen, Keith Krispin, and Roger Haber. Great directors and actors like Gwen Matthews, Joy Welker, Bob Conlon (for nearly twenty years Bob got roped into these performances), Laurie Powers and dozens more. I've had only one guy that I've been able to talk into just about anything, from dressing up like the Energizer Bunny™ to Leonard the Nerd. Thanks to Rick Krauser, who probably appeared in 75 percent of the following short dramas.

And there have been some wonderful encouragers: Robin and Pam, Bill and Jodi, Bob Rose, Frank and Sue, Carson and Sue, Lynn and Dorothy, the staff at Truer Truth, Brian, Brent, Steve, my in-laws, my parents, J.P., my old Bible study group, the Living Parable Drama teams at GCC, OCC, and Alpine, Nancy Haber, Fred and Diane, Jeff Hoyt, Buddy and Lisa and "Missen" Owen (although you've already joined our Lord I want you to know if it hadn't been for you our family never would have stayed in church).

I must mention that there were two special people who got dragged into more than their fair share of my mini-productions: my wife, Yvonne, and daughter, Becca. You two made it a lot easier for me than you think. My love and thanks to you both. But when it all comes right down to it I really need to thank the Lord. I'll not be so trite as to say that he *gave me* the dramas. But I will say that He placed the talent inside of me and led me to the experiences that nurtured it. I do hope that the following *Living Parables* bring the Lord the glory He deserves.

Table Of Contents

Introduction

"He spoke to them in parables." Jesus is considered the greatest speaker who ever lived. Why? He knew how to use stories. Stories are little slice-of-life pictures. And that's really what these *Living Parables* are all about. They are parables that help teach a biblical point. But they are not word parables as much as they are living parables.

Actors can add so much. They are the ones who make the words happy or sad. They snap out the funny punchlines or make that pregnant pause for emotional effect. They make these parables — living parables.

This collection reflects a few of the hundreds I've written. They target the seeker but give a good twist for the believer. I've tried not to "preach the message" but to create an introduction, a lead-in, a reference point for the message that might accompany it.

Because I have spent my time in both small and large churches, with or without stages and lighting, I've kept the props and scenery simple. It's all stuff you can find at home or at a local costume store.

Don't be afraid to change things around to give the sketch a closer tie to the message being taught. You might even find that you can write them yourself. Now, go make a "living parable."

Saturday Night At The Fights

Topic: Marriage, marriage battles, dysfunctional couples, relationships, arguments

Characters: Husband, wife, announcer, referee. Husband and wife are dressed in shorts and t-shirts with boxing gloves on

Scene: Boxing ring

Announcer: *(Can be offstage or dressed in a tux onstage)* Ladies and Gentlemen, welcome to the Palace's Saturday Night at the Fights. This evening's full card is brought to you by *Out of Focus on the Family,* the organization designed to create dysfunctional families. For our first bout of the evening: In this corner Joltin' John Smith. John weighs in at 200 pounds, stands 5' 7", is 41 years old, and is 37 and 37 in his career. His opponent is the one and only Wilma "Wildcat" Smith. Her age and weight are undisclosed. She also is 37 and 37 in the stats. And now let's go down to the ring to our referee.

Referee: Remember, Mrs. Smith and Mr. Smith, we have no rules for our fights. You both go in there and fire away. Now, go back to your corners and come out fighting at the sound of the bell.

(Return to corners, bell rings, they meet in the middle. With each line, the character throws a punch, mostly jabs until towards the end)

John: I can see your gray roots are showing through again. Of course, it amazes me that the dye can even cover your dingy gray mane.

Wilma: At least I've got hair.

John: But most of it is on your upper lip.

Wilma: Well, you've never been manly enough to grow any there.

John: What exercise program or diet plan are you trying this week for those cellulite pouches you carry around? When you walk down the street it looks like a motorcycle with saddle bags.

Wilma: By the way, I've changed your pet name from "Love Handles" to "Love Suitcases." Hey, did I miss something? When did the pear shape come into style? Or are you getting in shape for the Cardiac Arrest Olympics?

John: Maybe, if I got a decent home-cooked meal sometime. Maybe, if you weren't out shopping all day. Maybe, I would get something besides greasy, fatty, fried fast food.

Wilma: Maybe, if you made enough money for me to buy a nice enough house with a kitchen large enough to cook in. And with the way you throw the stuff down your throat, I'm surprised you haven't eaten a plate or two.

John: No one's holding you back from getting a job. I heard McDonald's™ is hiring "Seasoned Citizens" now.

Wilma: I couldn't do that. It would embarrass you if I brought home twice the salary you make. You would think that after twenty years at one job, you could get your own office or at least your own desk.

(John goes against the ropes)

John: It's probably because of all the love and encouragement I get at home. But then again, you're asleep when I leave for work and napping when I get home. So it really doesn't leave you much time to actually develop a relationship with me.

Wilma: Maybe, if you didn't whine in the morning about going to work and complain about work when you got home, I'd be awake. I might even listen. I might even care. (*Pause*) Nah!

John: You're starting to sound like your mother. *(Wilma staggers)*

Wilma: Maybe I should have listened to my mother when she said that you were a loser and that I shouldn't marry you. She was right. You're a loser! *(John staggers)*

John: Anyone in a partnership with you is bound to end up a loser. *(Wilma staggers)*

Wilma: Maybe you should just call the whole marriage off and try it with someone else. *(John drops to one knee)*

Sound effects: bell gong
(They stand and stare at each other in stunned silence. They start to back away from each other, showing hurt and fear)

Announcer: In a moment the referee will bring over his decision on who the winner is. While we wait I'll do a little color commentary. I thought for sure that Wilma had John on the ropes early with the jab about McDonald's™ paying twice as much as he makes. Mr. Smith's eyes rolled in his head for a second and then he came back strong and hard with that line about Wilma the Wildcat sounding like her mother. It would be hard for me to make a call on who won. Hold it; here comes the referee now.

(Ref opens slip of paper)

Referee: It's a draw. In this fight there are no winners. In this kind of fight there are only losers. And now for our next boxing match, Mr. and Mrs. You.

Exit

11

The Answering Machine

Topic: Serenity, stress, bills, hard times, troubles, caring God

Characters: One female

Props: Answering machine, table, chair, Bible, mail, letter opener

Scene: Living room

Character walks in with a briefcase, purse, bag of groceries, and a stack of mail in hand. As she comes in, the bag of groceries breaks. As she is leaning over to pick it up, the purse opens up and dumps its contents. When she tries to put her briefcase down, it opens up. Papers and files fall out. She finally gives up and sighs. Still holding the mail she starts to go through it.

Girl: Nothing but bills. Oh, wait. I think I've just won a million dollars. No, but I'm one of the finalists. Yeah, right, me and about 40,000 others. Doggone it. I'm sure I paid this bill. Can't they keep their records straight? I've been fighting with those-those-those *(looking for a clean word to use)* son-uva-guns since January. And they've messed it up again.

What's this? My car has been recalled. Two years too late, ya bunch of bozos. That piece of junk should have been recalled before it was made. That's the last time I buy a car that has the same name as my high school science teacher, good ol' Hugo Schlotz. *(Pause)* He said I'd never amount to anything. I guess he was right. Dead-end Doris, in a dead-end job.

Well, maybe the newspaper lottery called about that house I won. Believe me, the phone machine has got to be better than the mail.

(Pushes button)

Message 1: Doris, this is your mother. You promised to take me to the mall tonight. Where are you? I've already made dinner. It's your favorite — meatloaf. But make sure you bring your own ketchup. You know, I hate when you put ketchup on my meatloaf. Maybe your husband would still be around if you didn't use ketchup on your food. Listen, hon, Mom's got to go. See you about six and don't forget to bring some milk.

beep

Message 2: This is Rick Krauser calling from All America Realty. Ms. Shelley, starting July 1st, your rent is going up another $75. We're sorry for this inconvenience but the price of caring for the facility continues to grow and we need to pass some of those expenses on to you. Thank you.

beep

Message 3: Doris, this is Ed. Yes, that evil "ex" of yours. We need to talk. I think it's time for us to finally get out all the hostility between us. I'm coming over tomorrow morning. And this time, let me get a few words in edgewise.

beep

Message 4: *(Soft, soothing male voice)* Bad day, huh? Listen, I left a gift for you. It's on the chair. Open it up to the bookmark. *(Pause)*

Girl: What, who is this? How did someone get in? How did he know I was having a bad time of it?

Message 4: *(Continues)* Let's just say, I've been watching and I wanted to let you know I care. Bye.

Girl walks over and picks up the Bible. She opens the book to the bookmark and starts to read Psalm 23 (or the applicable Bible passage for the message). She weeps as she reads it. When she finishes it, she walks out carrying the Bible close to her heart.

Behind My Back

Topic: Reputation, ethics, lying, truth, testimony, deacons, leadership, services, giving, business practices

Characters: 3 males, 2 females

Scene: No scenery, only a stool

As the characters deliver their lines, they move right behind a seated Bill Johnson.

Bill Johnson: Hi, I'm Bill Johnson. I'm an upright guy. Good to my family and fair in all my business practices. I practice by the book. The good book. You know, the one that the Big Guy wrote. I'm listed in the Christian Yellow Pages. I even have one of those little fish in my logo. It's important that people know that I'm a part of the greater kingdom of God. We can certainly trust each other.

Businessman: Good old Bill Johnson. He certainly knows how to do business. He cuts corners so much that the doors won't shut on the building he put up for me. When I called him about it, he told me he'd have someone over that very day. It's been two months and my lawyer can't even get a return call. And I chose him because he went to my church. Fine example of the faith. Doesn't he know that when he does that he drags Christ's reputation down with him?

Bill Johnson: Why, just last week I had this fund-raiser babe from a charity in my office. I felt so bad for all those young kids that are struggling with the drug problems. I wanted to give a big fat donation, but business has been down lately. All I could do was pray with that sweet lady. I wished that I could help. My heart and prayers go out to those kids. There's got to be some way to help. Maybe I can use my influence as a deacon in the church to do something.

Fund-Raiser Female: I went to see Bill Johnson the other day. I'm with an organization that is trying to get drugs out of our neighborhood and out of our kids. He has been so vocal around town about the trouble that our kids are in. I heard him at a political function. He stressed how important his faith was and how important the kids were. I thought since he was such a pillar in the community, a good Christian man and a solid businessman, that I might be able to solicit some help — actually some funds. All of sudden I get this story about how bad business is. He wished he could help but it was a bad time. Now how could a guy driving around in a brand-new, very, very expensive car be having such a bad year? He talks like he's committed, but it looks like it's just talk.

Bill Johnson: You know this is a new day. A new age. Ethics are important in the businessplace again. I do my best to serve God and my customers in the best way I know how. I will bend over backwards for the customers and for my employees as well. Nobody is unimportant to Bill Johnson. Everybody matters to me because everyone matters to God.

Secretary: Sure, and the other day when International Wickets called because good, old, ethical Bill Johnson didn't finish the building on time, he had me tell them that he was out of town trying to find out why their lumber was being held up. The man is so quick with those little lies and all while he's lacing up his golf shoes.

Bill Johnson: As I said, the church is a very important part of my life. I'm on the Deacon Board. It means a lot to me knowing that I can serve God in this way. I have to make some tough decisions. I've gotta keep my eyes on the dollars, you know. God has called me to be a wise steward of his funds. The other day one of our committees requested funds to reach the neighborhood. They wanted to do a mailer, have a kids' club and a few other things. I thought it was a great idea. People need Christ and I'm the first one

15

to try to carry his torch to the community in any way I can. Some of the others felt we needed to put new carpet down in the Fellowship Hall first. It was a difficult decision but I know my convictions. The cause of Christ must go on.

Deacon or Deaconess: You should have seen Bill Johnson at the last Deacons' meeting. Laurie Peterson wanted to get her Outreach committee rolling again. Bill had led the battle to shut it down because it was too expensive. He felt that the church was large enough as it was and we needed things around here before we should waste money on the neighborhood. Of course, you should hear what he says about Missions. No one even tries that one anymore. Anyway Bill threw this tizzy fit about the Outreach ideas and about the Outreach Committee's poor leadership. Poor Laurie, she felt so defeated and beaten. I know Bill is concerned about the finances of the church and that's good, but sometimes he is so hard to get any new ideas through.

Bill Johnson: Hi, I'm Bill Johnson. I'm an upright guy. Good to my family and fair in all my business practices. I practice by the book. The good book.

Exit

McChurch

Topic: Food for spiritual health, growth, church, church attendance, Bible doctrine

Characters: 1 male, 1 female

Scene: Worksite. The two are having lunch from brown paper bags

Chuck: Well, I think that Julie and I have finally found a church.

Sally: Great! Where is it? What's it like?

Chuck: It's out in the subs.

Sally: North, south, west, northwest?

Chuck: North.

Sally: So, tell me about it. Harry and I are thinking of changing to something smaller. Worshiping with 5,000 of our closest friends isn't cutting it anymore. Tell me everything — what's its name?

Chuck: It's called McChurch.

Sally: No, seriously.

Chuck: I am serious. The pastor said he wanted something everyone could identify with. And who hasn't heard of McDonald's™? It has a lot of similarities to McDonald's™ too.

Sally: Like what? Drive-up windows?

Chuck: Yeah, how did you know? It's for people in a hurry. They can order a "sermonlite" and a side of praise music.

Sally: What's a side of praise music?

Chuck: Just a few bars of each song.

Sally: Any one in particular?

Chuck: Not really. I did notice that the song said something about loving one another.

Sally: You mean you went through the drive-up window.

Chuck: Sure, Julie and I had to make an early tee time, so we just hit the window. You know, a little religion is better than no religion. And the "sermonlite" was quite good. It was about respecting others and their cultural diversities.

Sally: I didn't hear any mention of Jesus in any of those things.

Chuck: Come to think of it, you're right. There wasn't any mention of him. But in the regular Sunday service he's mentioned in some of the menus. Of course, there is the new adults-only service, Archangel Deluxe.

Sally: Archangel Deluxe? Menus?

Chuck: Yeah, they've got different menus because some people want different things on Sunday. For instance, two weeks ago I got the vegetarian specialty. I think its called the McMeatless.

Sally: OK, what's that?

Chuck: I'm not sure, but I can assure you that it didn't have any substance. Guaranteed low calories and no nutritional content either.

Sally: And that's church? How do you expect to grow spiritually? Don't you want to have some spiritual power when you need it?

Chuck: Come to think of it, they seem to have everything but a power lunch there.

Sally: Can I ask you one question? Would you feel good about feeding a new baby nothing but fast food hamburgers?

Chuck: Don't be ridiculous. That would be a stupid way to grow a healthy child.

Sally: And ...

Chuck: And what? *(Looks at watch)* Well, lunchtime is just about over. Oh, yeah, I'll write out the directions to McChurch so you guys can try it.

Sally: Don't bother. I think there's a nice one near us *(or mention your own town)* we'll try. I heard they serve "Power Lunches" there.

Exit

The Mask

Topic: Sincerity, truthfulness, lying, deceit, ethics, slander

Characters: 2 females and 1 male

Scene: Anywhere

Note: Actors need to have photos taken early enough for the masks to be made. These should be enlarged on a color copier and glued on cardboard.

Harry: *(Behind mask)* Well, hello, Mary. It is so good to see you. What's been going on?
(Moves mask and talks to audience) I can't stand that woman. Why did I have to run into her here? There's no way to escape.

Mary: *(Behind mask)* Harry, I can't believe I bumped into you. I've been meaning to call you about that Johnson deal.
(To audience) Yeah, I was going to call that idiot. This bozo has just about ruined every deal I've tried to put together with him. I want nothing to do with him. Bumping into him is about as rewarding as a root canal.

Harry: *(Behind mask)* I was wondering about the Johnson thing. Is there any chance we can do lunch next week?
(To audience) That'll be great. I can watch her drool her food down her chin again. Working with her on a deal is a terrible experience. But then again, I'll probably be able to rip her off for quite a bundle. I could really feel bad about it all, but then again, hasn't God forgiven all those little indiscretions? If God forgives them, then why should I worry about them?

Mary : *(Behind mask)* Yeah, that's a great idea. I'll have my secretary call yours and set something up.
(To audience) Yeah, and I'll conveniently misplace the memo before I send it. If there is anybody in this world that justifies a little white lie, it's this guy.

Harry: *(Behind mask)* Great, I'll be waiting.
(To audience) That means I'll wait another year before I call back.

(Enter Jane)

Jane: *(Behind mask)* I can't believe that I'm seeing my two favorite people together. Mary, you look great. What did you do, lose weight, change your hair? I can't believe how great you look. And Harry, you look more successful than ever. Made another million, didn't you?
(To audience) Yeah, Mary has been trying to keep her weight down. It dropped alright. It dropped to her thighs. And Harry, he looks like a million bucks alright, all wrinkled and green.

Harry: *(Behind mask)* Jane, it is good to see you, but I need to run. Why don't you and your husband come up to the cabin with Josie and me? We'd love to get together again.
(To audience) Her husband just about ruined the last get-together. We were barbecuing and he knocked the whole thing into the pool. I lost about thirty bucks in steaks that day. But then again, Jane is not half bad looking. Maybe I should get together with her for a drink. What our mates don't know won't hurt them.

Mary: *(Behind mask)* I gotta run, too, but it was really great seeing you both again. I'll give you both a call.
(To audience) Glad I got out of that one. I feel so bad for Jane. She doesn't realize that people talk behind her back. She's lucky to have a friend like me that would never do that to her or, in fact, to anybody.

Exit

The Fool On The Hill

Topic: Spiritual power, prayer, wisdom, seeking

Characters: Woman and a guru

Sound Effects: Beatles, "Fool On the Hill"

Props: Long gray beard, robe, sandals on guru; hiking equipment on woman. Sermon notes on a clothespin that slides down a string from somewhere up above

Scene opens with Master Zing sitting in lotus position as the young woman approaches.

Woman: Master, I've finally found you. I've climbed three mountains, slept in the snow, ate roots from bushes, and finally I've discovered your place of meditation.

Master: Yes, my child. Help me to stand and we can talk. *(As he stands)* I've always hated that position. It makes my knees fall asleep. You know, this guru stuff isn't all it's cracked up to be. Sure, the walking on hot coals can warm your coddles, but this lotus sitting position is painful. Maybe I should get myself a nice beanbag chair. What do you think?

Woman: Master, that doesn't matter.

Master: That's because you weren't sitting there like a human pretzel.

Woman: Master, what matters is the answer to my question.

Master: Answers, smanswers. You don't need answers. What you need is a good cup of tea and a nice bagel. Or a week in the sun. Try a cruise.

Woman: I don't want that. I want answers.

Master: OK, ask away. No, wait. You aren't a Chicago Cubs fan, are you? Every year about this time, some nutty lady comes up here and asks me if the Cubs are going to win the pennant this year. I always say the same thing, "Anybody can tell you the answer to that one." *(Looks closely at her)* But you don't seem to be her, so go on. What is it you want to know?

Woman: I want to know how to harness spiritual power within.

Master: *(Under his breath)* Eat beans.

Woman: What was that, master?

Master: I said, isn't that keen. Now why is it you want to know how to harness peak power within?

Woman: I'm in the midst of a great spiritual battle. If I am going to win this struggle I must have the power.

Master: How much are you willing to pay for the answer?

Woman: What kind of question is that from a holy man?

Master: Hey, I gotta make a living somehow. Do you think that brown rice grows on trees? And do you have any idea what the rent is on a mountaintop spot? Lots of other gurus would love to have this place. It's prime real estate, you know.

Woman: I didn't bring any money. What can I give you?

Master: Got any fast food fries or burgers?

Woman: All-knowing one, how did you know that?

Master: Come on now, your knapsack's been stinkin' up the whole mountain.

Woman: If I give them to you will I receive this knowledge of how to harness spiritual power? *(She pulls fries out of her bag and gives them to him)*

Master: OK, first, I want you to close your eyes. Now, I want you to bend your knees until they both touch the ground *(she kneels)*. Now, bring your right palm over and let it touch your left. Intertwine your fingers *(as if praying)*. That's perfect. Finally, repeat after me, "Heavenly Father."

Woman: Master, this is a lot like prayer. I learned that as a kid. I didn't need to climb all the way up here to know about prayer. I could have simply read my Bible and it would've reminded me of prayer.

Master: I think you have finally discovered wisdom. Oh, and by the way, do you have any ketchup in that bag?

Exit

The Mission

Topic: Evangelism, soulwinning, evangelism programs, evangelism training, prayer

Characters: Captain, 2 Lieutenants, Sergeant, and several others as part of the army

Scene: Anywhere

Captain: All right, soldiers. The day has finally come, E Day. We are going to get out there and do evangelism. Caleb Company, you're going to hit (*your city name*). On the map here you'll see the areas marked with the heaviest concentration of sinners. Adam Company, you'll go into (*neighboring town or area*) and the surrounding areas under the cover of night. I want us to hit them fast and hard, then get out of there. Are there any questions?

Lt. Defazio: Yeah, Captain, I was wondering if we're going to get any training prior to the mission. We leave tonight but I'm not sure my people know what to do.

Captain: We have thousands of Gospel leaflets called tracts that your soldiers will carry with them. They are to leave one at every door and if they go into a restaurant they are to leave one for the waitress instead of a tip.

Sgt. Rockette: Captain, I've got a bunch of greenhorns. They've never been in a situation like this. What happens if they desert on me?

Captain: That's a possibility, Sergeant Rockette. They will face lots of opposition, and certainly some of them won't come back from the mission, but this has to be done or we'll lose this area to those godless humanists. And remember, it's like a domino game, once we lose a foot in one area we'll lose it all.

Lt. Burymore: What about my company, sir? We've been training for weeks with the four Spiritual Laws.

Captain: It's a special assignment for your guys. You're to hit the school campuses. Win those teachers. If we don't capture them before they unleash whole language concepts on our kids, then we'll lose the kids, too. Does everyone understand what they are to do?

Sgt. Rockette: What about (*name of wealthy section nearby*), sir?

Captain: The defenses are too high. We'll have to send in computer-guided mailings to do the job.

Lt. Defazio: What about air — I mean prayer — cover?

Captain: We've assembled every old grandma in the church. They'll be down on their knees binding the power of Satan all night. Now, everyone get out there and let's come back with some sinners.

Exit

Because It Is There

Topic: Obstacles, trials, troubles, preparation

Characters: 2 males

Scene: At the foot of the mountain

Sam: I can't believe it. Tomorrow we climb up the mountain and reach the top. This is a momentous occasion. This may go down in the history books. Do you know that no one has ever climbed this peak in recent history and no one has ever done it during the high wind season?

Harry: Why? Why do we do it?

Sam: Because it is there?

Harry: No, that's not it.

Sam: Then why?

Harry: For the endorsements.

Sam: Yes, the mountain-climbing equipment.

Harry: The mountain shoes.

Sam: The climbing ropes.

Harry: The camping gear.

Sam: The mountain-climber's trading cards.

Harry: The what?

Sam: Trading cards.

Harry: I don't think so. I don't think it'll ever get to that stage. Mountain climbing is not a national sport, you know?

Sam: Yeah, I guess you're right. OK, we know why we're doing it, but what do we know about our great nemesis, the mountain called "impossible" by all other climbers?

Harry: It's big.

Sam: It's high.

Harry: It has lots of rocks on it.

Sam: That white stuff up there might be snow.

Harry: I guess we know what we're up against. Now let's get some sleep and be ready for the morning's challenge.

Sam: OK, where's the tent?

Harry: I thought you grabbed it.

Sam: I told you to do it.

Harry: I wasn't about to carry that up here. Do you realize how difficult carrying that tent from the car would have been?

Sam: The car is only twenty feet away.

Harry: Forget it! I'm done. In fact, I'm tired already. Let's just quit.

Sam: All right, if that's what you want. We'll quit. *(Looks for car)* Where's the car?

Harry: It's right over there — where did it go?

Sam: Didn't you put the emergency brake on?

Harry: Was I supposed to?

Sam: When you're parked on a mountainside, it's always a good idea.

Harry: You know, I don't think we were really up to this. So what do we do?

Sam: Let's walk back to the lodge and tell everyone we made it halfway up and were caught in a rock slide.

Harry: Good idea, that ought to impress the babes.

(They high-five each other as they exit)

Sam: You know, we ought to throw some dirt on ourselves so we look like we were caught in a rock slide.

Exit

It's A Dog's Life

Topic: Friendship, relationship, appreciation, responsibility,

Characters: 2 dogs (in costumes)

Scene: The backyard

Prince: Hey, Dutch, I'm glad you could come over.

Dutch: No problem. You know as long as there's that hole under the fence, I can get out any time I want.

Prince: Doesn't your master ever fill it up?

Dutch: I don't think it bothers him that I get out. He's pretty liberal in how he treats me, you know.

Prince: Yeah, I guess that's OK. By the way, it looks like you've been losing weight. New diet? He's got ya on Cycle 4 now, doesn't he?

Dutch: Prince, the old guy's been gone so much that I'm glad if he gets out to feed me at all. I've been dining out a lot lately.

Prince: (*Using a French accent*) Chez Garbage?

Dutch: Oui, oui, mon sewer. I have eaten from zee finest garbage pails in zee city.

Prince: That's too bad. Maybe I can rustle up a little grub around here. All I gotta do is push my dish around and the old guy gets the hint. How about if we go Italian? Last night I had pupparoni pizza and the night before dog dish pizza. I'm sure there's something good in there.

Dutch: That's OK, I stopped at a fast food place and picked up a little something.

Prince: I'm always scared to eat there. I'm afraid it might be a relative or something.

Dutch: Beggars can't be choosers.

Prince: I suppose.

(Awkward silence; they both scratch)

Prince: So what do you think happened? I mean you two used to be inseparable friends. He took you everywhere. I don't think I ever saw his car go down the road without your head out its window.

Dutch: I don't really know. We just quit hanging out together. He hasn't thrown a ball or a stick to me in over a year.

Prince: Is that dog or human years?

Dutch: Human. Anyway, it bothered me at first but I'm kinda getting used to it. You know, we used to roll on the floor and play a lot. Of course, the driving around was fun. We had a great time when he gave me a bath. He always ended up as wet as I was. I remember one time we took this trip to the lake and I played fetch in the water for hours. We really had some great times. But he's changed.

Prince: So what do you think went wrong?

Dutch: He takes me for granted. Does he ever think about all the times I protected the house? What about the guy that carries those funny pieces of paper around every day and puts them in the box out front? Who scares him away every day? Not the old man. Even though he says he hates getting that junk from him, my master never chases him away. That's my job. And what kind of thanks do I get? None.

31

Prince: I know what you mean.

Dutch: Or all the times that he gets impatient with me when I mess up a little. Hey, dogs have accidents, you know. It doesn't seem like a big deal to me, but he goes nuts when I do — well, you know — in the house. Or the day I jumped up and tried to help him type on the computer. I mean, a dog has got to keep up with technology.

Prince: Things sound real bad.

Dutch: I guess what hurts the worst is that we just don't hang out together any more. Dog, I miss those times.

Prince: Sometimes that happens around here, too.

Dutch: What do you do?

Prince: Gotta love those humans even then. They'll come around.

Dutch: You've got a lot of insight into humans. You seem to understand them pretty well.

Prince: Understanding is the beginning of any good friendship. I love the old guy and I love his family as well because we're all part of the same family. You might say that I'm the man's best friend. We've got a special relationship. I'm loyal and he feeds me. What could be better?

Dutch: You got it.

Prince: Say, how 'bout us drinking a gallon of water each and roaming the neighborhood?

Dutch: No, I think I'm headin' back home. The old guy could probably use his best friend hanging around.

Prince: Great, see ya later then.

Exit

Get With The Program

Topic: Ambitions, organization, potential, career, budgeting

Characters: Husband, wife and computer voice offstage

Scene: Home office, computer on a desk

Paul: Honey, Penny, Honey. Come in here. I've got to show you the new program I got for the computer and the new sound chip. This thing is so great. Man, this thing will do everything for us.

Penny: *(Enters from door)* What was all that yelling about? ·

Paul: I got this new program and a sound chip to go with it. This thing is so great. This program can help us get our lives organized. It will do our budget, our schedule, our ...

Penny: Can it make dinner?

Paul: *(Playfully)* Can you?

Penny: That's exactly where I'm heading right now.

Paul: Let me just show you a few things. OK, I double click on the icon.

Penny: Who's the guy in the icon? Kinda cute, white beard, knowing eyes. I feel like I once looked into that face many years ago. Somehow I've forgotten who it is.

Paul: It's somebody. *(Frustrated at her tangent)* I don't know. Don't ask those stupid questions. Now watch.

Computer: Welcome to MacDivine (PCDivine). I am here to help you organize your life to reach its peak potential.

Paul: Pretty neat, huh?

Penny: Yeah, this is better than the Mike Ditka Football Fantasy game that you're always playing.

Computer: Please choose your category by voice command. Would you like to explore your budget; your recreational time; your time management; Christmas ideas; or career opportunities ...

Penny: Budget!

Peter: We can do that later. I'm in the midst of my midlife crisis.

Penny: Bad day at work, hon? *(Rubs his shoulders)*

Peter: Every day seems to be a bad day at work. I feel like I've already accomplished everything I can. I can't go any higher. I'm ready for a change.

Penny: My husband, the Michael Jordan of accounting.

Peter: I'm serious. I want to look at Career Opportunities. OK, computer, Career Opportunities.

Computer: Thank you for choosing Career Opportunities. Let's begin. MacDivine will guide you through several possible areas. Let's begin with your interests. Are you looking to your job to give you significance in your social arena?

Peter: No.

Penny: Be honest now, you know it means a lot to you that you own your own accounting firm. In fact, that's all you used to talk about.

Peter: Yeah, but if I say that then the computer is going to tell me to go back to accounting.

Penny: Be honest, that's all I'm saying.

Peter: *(To computer)* Yes!

Computer: Thank you, the next question is: Are you looking to your job to give you the security that you and your family need?

Peter: Isn't everyone?

Computer: That does not compute.

Peter: Sorry. I just meant that isn't everyone looking to their jobs to provide them the security they need?

Computer: Is it ever secure?

Peter: Well ...

Penny: Try to remember why you went into your own business.

Peter: Because I lost my job at Dewey, Cheatum and Howe. Listen, I'm getting a little tired of a computer program analyzing me this way.

Penny: I wasn't the one who bought it.

Peter: OK, OK. Isn't it time for dinner yet?

Penny: Nope, I want to do the one about budget.

Computer: Thank you for choosing Budget. We'll begin with your giving to God. How much do you return to God each week or month?

Penny: Well, ah, there must be some kind of bug in this program. *(Pause)* Peter, I'm getting a little hungry.

Peter: Me, too.

Penny: Dinner will be ready in a few minutes.

Paul: Well, I've got a few more things to do on the computer for work, then I'll be right in *(double clicks)*.

Computer: Welcome to Asteroids, a game of challenge and skill.

Paul: Now, this is what a computer is for.

Exit

Born Leader

Topic: Unselfishness, head of church, leadership, ministry teams, servanthood, dictator

Characters: One male and voice offstage

Scene: Man at a desk

Man: OK, now how should I start this speech to my ministry team? My peons. No, that won't do. *(Crumbles up paper and tosses it on each mind change)* How about, you little people better listen up. Nah, won't work. Listen up, I'm the ministry leader and I've got something to say. Maybe. It's just so difficult to be a key leader in the church. I've got to get this group to do what I want them to do.

Voice Offstage: You mean, to do what I want them to.

Man: What's that? What'd you say?

Voice: I said, "To do what I want them to."

Man: Is that you, Pastor?

Voice: A little higher up than that.

Man: You don't sound like my wife.

Voice: Still a little higher.

Man: My secretary.

Voice: *(A little angry)* No!

Man: Listen, I'm not very good at this. Can you give me a hint or two?

Voice: I didn't have this much problem with that hardhead Moses.

Man: Charlton Heston?!

Voice: I'm going to make it real simple for you. This is the Lord speaking.

Man: Hold it! Hold it! I'm not sure that I want to have God speaking to me. People get into trouble that way.

Voice: I assure you that this is only a short visit. And I promise not to bother you again. OK?

Man: Yeah, sure, that's OK. But why are you bothering, I mean, talking to me now?

Voice: Because you have this whole idea of ministry wrong. You are not to lord it over the others that I have called you to lead. A leader needs to be a servant. Not a dictator.

Man: But these people have got to do what is best for the church.

Voice: And who decides what is best for the church?

Man: Can I have a few hints again?

Voice: Me. The church is my body. I place the leaders. You are there to serve and minister to others, not to have others do your bidding.

Man: Yeah, well, you should tell that to the Assistant Pastor *(or whoever takes a joke the best)*. What a dictator he is. I think it's short man's syndrome. OK, I think I'm getting the drift here. My team needs to decide how we can serve you, and then as their leader

I have to be the (*choking sound*) servant of all. This is going to be hard. I'm not sure that I like that kind of servanthood.

Voice: It's the only kind I like. And wouldn't you rather please me and hear me say, "Well done, my good and faithful servant"?

Man: Gotcha.

Voice: Well, that's it. It wasn't so painful, was it?

Man: Well, actually, is it possible for us to get together again? I think I need a few more of these discussions.

Voice: Sure, I'm in the Book.

Man: The book? Oh, the Book! Gotcha.

Exit

Fruit Or Twinkies?

Topic: Fulfillment through the fruit of the spirit

Characters: Husband and wife

Scene: The kitchen of the home of Bill and Sarah. As the scene opens Bill is carrying several different items of food to a table at center stage. He begins to munch on something when Sarah calls from offstage

Sarah: Bill, what are you doing now?

Bill: I finished patching that hole in the bedroom so I'm going to have a snack. But I don't know what I want.

Sarah: *(Still offstage)* Try some fruit.

Bill: No, no. Fruit isn't what I want. I just have that empty feeling inside. Maybe a Snickers™ will do it. Peanuts, caramel, and a cup of milk in every bar. That ought to take care of my empty feeling. *(He takes a bite)* Nah! I wish I could find something that would satisfy me. *(He rummages through the food some more)* A Twinkie™. Now this is what it will take to fill that empty spot in the old stomach. *(Just as he takes a bite Sarah walks in)*

Sarah: Did you find what you were looking for?

Bill: *(He is chewing on the Twinkie™)* I tried a Snickers™ and a Twinkie™ and neither one of them seemed to do it.

Sarah: How about some fruit?

Bill: Oh, come on now. What makes you think that fruit would be the thing that I need? Personally I feel that what I need is something a little more like — ah — potato chips.

Sarah: Bill, this exasperates me. You will try just about everything in the house to fill up that great empty void you call a stomach except for fruit. Fruit is known to help you cope with this lacking more than any other item out there in the supermarket. How about a nice piece of fruit? *(She pulls a pear out of the basket on the table)*

Bill: Sarah, please get off this kick. For years now I have been researching every known food group to man.

Sarah: Junk food groups.

Bill: OK, but at least I'm trying to discover what is worthwhile to eat out there and what it takes to fill the void within me and maybe just maybe I am gonna find the one thing that could make life, well, worthwhile for everyone.

Sarah: I'm telling you that you don't need all that junk food to find something worthwhile to fill that void you call a stomach. Fruit would do it. Trust me.

Bill: Let's say that I toss my cookies *(He throws one in a bag on the table)* and switch to fruit, what do I gain?

Sarah: Well, it isn't so much what you'll gain as it is what you can give.

Bill: If I add fruit to my life I don't gain as much as I can give? This doesn't make sense to me.

Sarah: OK, you see, if you have fruit in your life you are better able to deal with all the garbage that comes your way. If you keep trying to fill the needs in your life with senseless, empty things

41

then you don't have all that you should have. Especially when you need to really exercise.

Bill: That makes sense.

Sarah: Then how about some fruit?

Bill: Sounds great. What should I start with?

Sarah: How about this? *(She hands him an apple)*

Bill: No thanks, the last guy that took one of those from his wife lost his job as a gardener.

Exit

Here I Am, Lord; Send Somebody Else!

Topic: Missions, inner-city, summer missions

Characters: 4

Scene: Twilight Zone-ish

Character 1: Me, go overseas! You've got to be kidding me. First of all, I can't even speak a foreign language. Even worse, I have no language aptitude at all. I guarantee I have absolutely nothing in that department. I failed pass/fail French class. I don't even know the difference between French bread and French toast. Forget it. If there was a chance to do something in English I'd be the first one there, but I don't think that is what I'm supposed to do. Actually, I'm not sure I know what God wants me to do. I want to serve him. I want to do something that will be significant for his kingdom, but I'm a little lost on what that is. I'm not sure you would call me a public speaker. Yeah, I pray aloud, but God is a lot more tolerant than the people who would have to listen to me preach. So what can I do? Nothing of any value in missions. I'm just a carpenter, I work with my hands. God can't use me, can he?

Character 2: Every morning, in my devotions, I ask God what it is that he wants me to do. If God wants me on the mission field then I think he would say so. And you know, I don't get any response. I guess I'm not called to missions. It's as simple as that.

(Turns to leave and then turns back)

I haven't been honest with you. I'm not sure that I really want to go to the mission field. I don't feel called to any particular foreign field. But I do feel a burden to use the gifts that God has given me to reach people that need to hear about our Lord. But what can I do? I get nervous at the thought of jumping on an airplane or some ocean tanker to head off for Boinga-Boinga Land. Is there anyway to get the mission field to come to me?

Character 3: What? Me on the mission field? Forget it! I'm getting too old for that. Besides, I have kids in school that want to graduate from their high school right here in this town. I've got a good job and I'm in line for a promotion. Big money, if you know what I mean. I'm a deacon at our church and I hold the very prestigious job of Sunday School Superintendent. I'm afraid there is just too much stacked against me to go off to the mission field. Don't get me wrong, I think that missions are really important. There just isn't any way that I can serve on a foreign field. I feel God needs me right here. If God were to call me, what would I do? I'd say, "Here I am Lord, send somebody else." I'm afraid that foreign missions will have to wait. Right now, I just can't get involved in something that takes me so far away from my life as I know it.

Character 4: *(Character 4 should be from an inner-city area. Character 4 walks out among the three other characters)* I've been listening to what you've been saying. Friends, the mission field isn't just overseas. The mission field is anywhere that people need Christ. Currently one of the neediest areas is the city. Anybody can get involved there. You speak the language, you don't have to fly there, and your family can stay where they are as you labor for God with the talents, craftsmanship, and gifts he's given you. Remember the *Action* is in the cities.

(The four characters all walk off together as if they have discovered something fantastic and are excited about it)

Lights

Pass The Buck

Topic: Responsibility of knowing Christ, salvation, temptation, evangelism

Characters: One male or female, a devil, and an angel, the same sex as the lead character

Scene: Moody, dark lighting

Devil: Confused again? Let me help you.

Angel: Stop it, you're the one who confuses him all the time. He needs to make a decision about this thing and he needs to do it soon.

Devil: I don't know if he needs to do it or not. I mean, there's plenty of time and no decision is OK.

Angel: Wrong, no decision is the same as the wrong decision when it comes to this question. You know about him, you've heard it. Come on, friend. What should you do with Jesus?

Character: Sure, I've heard all about him. I used to go to this place when I was a kid. You know, this lady would sit with us and tell us all about him. I thought I knew everything. I enjoyed it all, but I think I liked the cookies more than the lessons. I even went to one of those camps in the summer. I heard it all again and again there from some guy. So I knew it all. I had the knowledge but, I wonder, is that enough to make me accountable? I mean, did I really know enough? Wasn't there something else that I should know?

Devil: That's right, there's always plenty more for you to know. I mean, those letters written about him are filled with contradictions.

They would totally confuse you, so you don't need to read them. Trust me.

Angel: Trust him, are you kidding me? This guy is trying to get you to stay away from the decision.

Character: Later on, I went to this meeting and everybody was talking about him. You see, I thought that I needed to know more, and I wanted to know more because with knowledge comes — ah — ah ... *(Pause)*

Angel: Responsibility.

Character: Responsibility.

Devil: Great, now you're listening to him again. Don't you realize that everything he's saying you learned back in Sunday School? It's kids' stuff. The knowledge you gained there isn't what life is made of. Life is filled with cold, hard facts.

Character: So I knew, but what was I to do with all this knowledge? At first I thought, well, that's all right for somebody else. I mean, that may be fine for you to be one of those fanatics, but I need to live in the real world. I don't want that pie in the sky thing. I deal in reality, cold, hard facts, and I'm not sure this is cold, hard facts, is it? You can be the judge in this situation for yourself. If you think that it's true then I guess it is true — for you.

Angel: *(To devil)* What did you do? Teach him that all things are relative?

Devil: Yeah, not bad, huh? I mean, what is truth anyway? Ha ha ha.

Character: Think about it. I'm being asked to judge whether something is true or not. What's truth? Is it true only if I can feel it; or only if I can see it; or only if science can prove it? I agree with some of that, and I'm not sure that I have enough to make a decision. Hey, making a decision about truth is difficult. It's hard to tell what is real and what isn't in this world.

Angel: Make a decision and get on with things!

Devil: Don't worry about making a decision. You're pretty good the way you are. You never killed anybody, did you?

Character: Listen, I know what you're thinking. You think that I should just make a decision and get on with things. In a way I have. I've done the best I could with what was presented to me. Is that enough? Look, I never killed anyone. I've done my best. Besides, if I'm not positive that something is true then I shouldn't make a decision. That would be hypocritical.

Devil: That's right, you had nothing to do with it. I mean, there were a lot of people who didn't consider it true about him. Didn't you just go with the ...

Character: Flow, that's right. I just went with the flow. Isn't truth what everybody believes? I've been told that if one person tells you you're a horse, then ignore it. If two people tell you that you're a horse, look for hooves, and if three people tell you you're a horse, then buy a saddle. The Good Book says that there were people screaming and yelling that Jesus wasn't the one.

Angel: But you still had the knowledge. Remember all those Sundays you spent in that room? What did that teacher tell you?

Character: I need to receive him. He died for me. Oh, come on now. *(Rolls eyes)* What in the world am I saying? I had nothing to do with his death. Look at these hands, they are clean. There's no blood on them. I didn't drive the nails or spear in. I had nothing to do with it, so get off my back. It's their problem; *(points to congregation)* they need to make the decision.

Devil: That's it, my friend, pass the buck.

Angel: Knowledge breeds responsibility. What are you going to do with Jesus?

(Character pulls a dollar out of his pocket.)

Character: Look for someone to pass this to.

Exit

Everybody Plugs Into Something

Topic: Salvation

Characters: Narrator, Harry, personal trainer, businessperson, God *(God should be dressed in all white)*. Trainer, businessperson, and God are holding electrical receptacles from a hardware store *(Put the plug covers on them)*

Scene: Twilight Zone-ish

Narrator: Harry is a nice guy. He's always done everything the way one is supposed to. Harry never hurt anyone — intentionally. He tried to never lie or cheat. I guess you would say that Harry is an all-around nice guy. But, like it is for everyone in life, a time came when he felt like something was missing. He had been running on his own personal power for a long time and now it had run out.

(Harry is sitting on a chair, slumped over. There is a plug coming out of his back. It is long enough to reach all the other characters and still perform the actions he needs to make.)

Harry looked around for something to get plugged into. He thought maybe it might be his health that was going. You know how it is when you get into your forties. First the legs go, then the eyes and finally — ugh — the hair. Maybe, if he plugged into a good exercise program …

(Harry walks the plug over to the Aerobics outlet and plugs in. Immediately, Harry starts to exercise along with the Aerobics character to a Jane Fonda tape. They go through fifteen seconds of exercise, then Harry begins to run down. Harry pulls the plug and collapses, exhausted, into his chair.)

Harry rethinks his exercise program. Possibly, he should have gone into this aerobics thing a little more slowly. But that's OK, because before he can even say ...

Harry: ... man, am I beat!

Narrator: Harry discovers another plug. It's the money machine.

(Harry plugs himself into the Money Machine outlet. Harry immediately grabs his briefcase and acts like he is trying to close a deal. He pulls charts out, paperwork, and more. Money Machine looks at Harry and shakes his head.)

Rejection! That's hard for old Harry. What's left? Harry wants to plug into something that will fulfill him. He wants something to make him happy again. He wants something that will empower him, but nothing is left, he says. Harry!

Harry: Yeah, what do you want?

Narrator: There's one more plug over there.

(The God plug is sitting, smiling, patiently waiting. He waves to Harry.)

Harry: I tried that one before.

Narrator: When?

Harry: Back when I was a kid, I went to Sunday School, AWANA, Youth Group, and I even sang in the choir.

Narrator: But did you ever get plugged in? Did you ever trust him as your power source?

Harry: Well, I heard everybody talking about trusting Christ, but I thought that if I was good enough ...

Narrator: ... and ran on your own power?

Harry: Yeah, that's it.

Narrator: So did it work?

Harry: No.

Narrator: Harry carried his plug over to the God receptacle and plugged in.

(Harry is excited. He feels the power and smiles. Harry and God go off the stage with their arms around one another.)

Narrator: It looks like Harry has finally tapped into the right power source for his life. What about you? What are you plugged into?

Exit

Hard Sale

Topic: Biblical truth, cults

Characters: Salesman, man, woman

Scene: A kitchen table

Salesman: OK, so what do you say? Which one will it be?

He: We can't just make up our minds like that. We need more time ...

She: More information ...

He: More research ...

She: More reasons ...

Salesperson: Exactly what is it that you think that you need? I have explained everything that I can.

She: We can't just make a decision as important as the church we attend or the faith that we believe in a few minutes.

Salesperson: What more do you want to know?

He: Who's the head of this thing anyway?

Salesperson: What difference does it make who the head is? What's important is what's in the teaching.

She: But if the head is wrong then the teaching is going to be wrong. If the teaching is wrong then we are going to get into big trouble when we get to heaven and God wants to know why we think we should get in.

He: We also want to know what you think is the pathway to heaven. Is it faith? Is it works? Is it faith plus works? Is it none of the above? Or do I have to stand on a street corner handing out magazines ...

She: And shave my head ...

He: And go without meat ...

Salesperson: This is amazing. For hundreds of years people have not been asking these questions. Why are you starting now? It is not that difficult. You just believe what I have told you. Keep it simple and don't worry your pretty little heads about all that stuff. Let me handle that end for you.

He: What do you mean? This is the crux of the universe and you want us to just accept it because you've said it. I'm afraid that is not the way it is going to go, sport. We want real answers before we can make real decisions.

Salesperson: All right, if that's the way you are, then just forget it. I gave you a chance and you have turned away from it. *(He stamps his feet two times and dust flies)*

He: Honey, maybe we've been too hasty with her (him). Could you wait another minute? I think we need to confer one last time. *(To each other, off to the side)* OK, what if they're right and we are wrong? If he/she is right, then we're lost.

She: What are you suggesting?

He: I think we need to cover our bases a little better.

She: Go ahead.

He: Why don't we take a little bit of theirs and a little bit of ours and mix them together, and then we can be covered under both systems?

53

She: I think that will work. I like their freedom to do what they want during the week.

He: I like that we don't feel as if we need to give physically, emotionally, or financially to the system. No investment, just withdrawal.

She: This could work out well. Let's mix it all together.

He: *(To salesperson)* We've decided to take only a part of the package. None of that commitment or faith stuff for us. What will it cost?

Salesperson: I'm afraid that it will cost you nothing now but everything in the distant future.

Exit

Is It Really Worth It?

Topic: Easter services, inviting neighbors to church, cost of salvation, Christ's payment on the cross

Characters: Husband and wife

Scene: Living room or family room

Wife: I was reading in the paper that two of those churches that are near our house are having special Easter Services.

Husband: (*Reading the mail*) Yeah, so what?

Wife: So, I'd like to go.

Husband: Come on. Why? Why give up a quiet, peaceful Sunday morning to hear some preacher whine about how much money the church needs and how terrible cable TV is for the morality of our nation? It just ain't worth it.

Wife: Not worth it? What do you mean? This isn't just any Sunday. This is Easter Sunday! Do you realize what Easter is all about?

Husband: Yeah, chocolate bunnies, colored eggs, and baskets overflowing with candy. I hope you have mine fixed already. You know what my favorite is?

Wife: I can't wait for your pearl of wisdom.

Husband: I like those chocolate crosses, and, my dear, that is all the closer I'm getting to this Jesus because it just isn't worth it.

Wife: Maybe you don't understand what Easter is all about. Well, then, do you see any value in Good Friday? Do you even know what happened on Good Friday?

Husband: Sure, I saw the movie. Bing Crosby is this priest, you see, and he ...

Wife: No, that isn't it.

Husband: I know. I was just kidding. It was Charlton Heston. *(Laughing)*

Wife: *(She throws a newspaper at him)* Oh, you are so frustrating. You don't know, do you?

Husband: I know it isn't worth my going to church in the middle of the week.

Wife: How about Easter then?

Husband: No, it isn't worth the time.

Wife: If you only knew what it was all about, maybe then you would feel it was worth it. If you could get it through your thick head that Good Friday was probably the most expensive day in history ...

Husband: Most expensive day in history! Well, I'm glad I didn't have to pay the bill then.

Wife: That's right. You didn't and you couldn't have. Only Jesus could do it.

Husband: Do you think I could get him to pay my Visa bill as well?

Wife: OK, I've had it. I'm going to church Easter with or without you.

Husband: You sure are touchy lately. I think that Jane Fonda exercise tape has rattled your brains. You better switch to low-impact aerobics. This whole subject isn't worth us arguing over.

Wife: Ugh!

Husband: *(Reads paper)* Hey, babe, listen to this. There is going to be a funny car race at the *(local auditorium or drag strip)* to-morrow. Now this is worth the effort to get there. I love to see those guys go whipping around that track. Vrmmmm! *(Acts as if he is driving)*

Wife: Funny cars are worth it, but Jesus isn't?

Husband: Well, uh, yeah. I guess so.

Wife: You know, you have your priorities in the wrong place, boy.

Husband: *(Ignores her for a few minutes)* Are there any of those jelly beans left?

Wife: In the cupboard, but you already ate all the black ones.

Husband: Where?

Wife: I'm not sure it's worth it to show you.

Husband: Honey, a great love like mine is worth it.

Wife: But God's great love isn't?

Husband: Are we back on this God thing again? You sound like a broken record. I just don't think it's worth it.

(She stomps out)

Husband: Wait a second; let's talk about this.

Exit

57

Just A Mistake

Topic: Self-esteem, encouragement, fortitude, vision

Characters: Dad, Mom, teenage daughter

Scene: Dinner table

Mom: OK, everybody, it's time for dinner!

(Father and daughter enter)

Dad: Great, I'm so hungry I could eat a horse.

Mom: Good, because that's what we're having.

Daughter: Mom, that's gross.

Dad: C'mon now, honey, I thought that was pretty funny. I mean, for your mother.

Mom: Well, it's going to get cold so have a seat.

(They sit down at the table)

Dad: Little angel, would you pray for the meal?

Daughter: Rub-a-dub-dub, thanks for the grub.

Mom: Now, that's out of line.

Dad: That's my family, a real laugh a minute. Let's dig in and eat cause I'm so hungry I could eat a …

Mom and Daughter: Horse.

Dad: OK, so it's a bad joke and I use it all the time. I'll try to purge that from my dinner conversation. And speaking of dinner conversation, did you try out for the school play?

Daughter: No way, all those other kids are too good. I would just get lost in the shuffle. Mary Louise Fenster is going to get the lead again. She always does. She's been taking classes at that college in town in the summer.

Mom: Do you want to take classes too?

Daughter: I don't think so. I just don't have any talent in those areas.

Dad: I think you're selling yourself short. I think you're a great actress. I don't see why you can't be in the movies, if you wanted.

Mom: Yeah, your father is right. You are very special and I think you should go out there and show them what you've got.

Daughter: I don't think I have it.

Dad: Please try, OK?

Daughter: OK.

Dad: I forgot to ask how the election went at the Women's Group. Did you get the presidency?

Mom: No way. I'm not as good as those other people. I feel like a big mistake next to some of those women. Two of them are doctors, three are lawyers, and not one of them drives a beater like mine to the meetings.

Daughter: Mom, you're no mistake.

Mom: Well, I feel like one.

Dad: That isn't the way I see it. You are a winner. In fact, you are a miracle.

Mom: Anyway, I didn't even run for the office. I left that for someone better than me.

Daughter: Oh, by the way. I need a new dress for the big banquet at the church.

Mom: No problem. Since your dad asked for the raise today at work, we should be able to do that easily.

Dad: *(Chokes on food)* Well, maybe we should talk about this dress thing.

Mom: You didn't ask for the raise?

Dad: Not exactly. I don't feel like I deserve it.

Daughter: Why?

Dad: All those other people in the office are so much better than I am. I don't think that I deserve a raise.

Daughter: But, Dad, you're always saying how the office couldn't operate without you.

Mom: She's right, honey. Besides, you're so special. I think you're a miracle, too.

Dad: I'm glad everyone else around here thinks I am, because I feel like a big zero.

Daughter: Yeah, Dad, you're the greatest.

Dad: Do you really think I'm mistaken about myself?

Mom and Daughter: Absolutely!

Dad: OK, then tomorrow I ask for the raise. And what about you two? Are you going to try out for the play and run for the Women's Group presidency?

Daughter: No way, I'm a big zero.

Mom: Me, too.

Dad: I guess I don't really need that raise. We can make it on what I bring in.

Daughter: Yeah, I don't even deserve to be with all those great kids at church. They're so spiritual and I can't even remember John 3:16. Forget the dress.

Mom: Dessert anyone? It's not that good but it's filling.

Dad: I just don't deserve a family as good as this.

Lights

1-900-MIDLIFE

Topic: Midlife crisis, aging, introduction to the life of Abraham, faithful living

Characters: 1 doctor, 5 callers offstage on a microphone

Scene: Radio studio or a TV studio with a chair, end table and a telephone

Doctor: Hello, you're on Midlife. How can I help you?

Caller 1: Well, I just turned forty and I was thinking of leaving my wife for two twenty-year-olds. What do you think?

Doctor: I don't think you're wired for 220. Next. Welcome to Midlife.

Caller 2: Hi, Doctor. I listen to your show all the time and, well, I never thought that I'd actually be on it.

Doctor: Surprise, surprise. Here you are. Now, how can I help you?

Caller 2: Well, I've been feeling a little empty lately.

Doctor: Have you tried eating something?

Caller 2: I don't mean in my stomach. It's more in my soul.

Doctor: Continue.

Caller 2: My job is going nowhere. Even though I'm one of the vice presidents, I feel like this isn't what I really want to do with my life. I need some kind of change.

Doctor: Have you tried a sports car?

Caller 2: No.

Doctor: Go get one!

Caller 2: But … *(he's cut off)*

Doctor: Next.

Caller 3: Can I have a pizza with double cheese, pepperoni, and sausage to go?

Doctor: What?

Caller 3: Ain't this Gino's Pizzeria?

Doctor: *(Rolling eyes)* Next. You're on Midlife.

Caller 4: Doctor, something strange has happened to me. It's hard to describe.

Doctor: You can tell me, I'm a doctor.

Caller 4: I think I'm turning into my father. I'm starting to make his noises. When I get up in the morning, I go "Ohhh" just like he did. I also find myself falling asleep in the chair after dinner. Just the other day, I said to my kids, "Do you want a spanking?" Like they'd say, "Yes, Dad, I was meaning to ask for one. Could I have it now, before dinner?" Doctor, I'm becoming my dad.

Doctor: I think it's just repressed anger from not getting that bicycle when you were a kid.

Caller 4: That doesn't make any sense.

Doctor: Are you questioning me? I'm a doctor!

Caller 4: No, but …

Doctor: Get off the line and let people talk who want to be helped. Next.

Caller 5: Hi, my name is Abraham. I'm in my midlife and God just told me to pack up and leave my home, but he won't tell me where I'm supposed to go.

Doctor: First of all, are you sure it was God?

Caller 5: Yes, I'm sure.

Doctor: Next time you see him, ask him a question for me?

Caller 5: OK, what is it?

Doctor: Will the *(local sports team)* win the *(Pennant, World Series, Super Bowl, NBA Championship)*?

Caller 5: What does that have to do with my midlife?

Doctor: Nothing, but I've got twenty bucks riding on it. OK, now let me get back to your problem. So, God said get going, and you don't know where you're going?

Caller 5: Yes, that's right. And the tough thing is that I'm in my midlife and I want to do the right thing. Do I press ahead without more information or do I just do the safe thing?

Doctor: I'm sorry, but that's all the time we have. See you again tomorrow on 1-900-MIDLIFE. And remember, if you want answers to your midlife questions, you better read the manual. Good night.

The Invitation

Topic: Inviting others, evangelism, encouragement, caring

Characters: Three women on the phone

Scene: A table will be set up with a phone on it. Characters 2 and 3 will have their backs to the congregation. Each character's original spot will be marked with tape with her number on it. As the characters rotate, they move to the next spot in a counterclockwise circle. #1 will be standing next to the phone as the lights come up. When she finishes her lines the three move in a counterclockwise way until #2 is standing next to the table facing the congregation. She then picks up the phone. When she finishes, then #3 circles counterclockwise again until #3 is standing next to the table facing the congregation. As she finishes, the lights go out and the three characters exit

#1: *(She dials the phone)* Oh, hi, Mary. This is Margaret. How's things going? *(Pause)* And the kids, how are they? *(Pause)* Oh, I know what you mean, we keep running Billy back and forth from game to game, too. It is certainly getting old, but I found something that's really helped. *(Pause)* No, it isn't gagging and tying him. In fact, it would be great for you. You need it. No, no, I insist that you get involved with this. I won't take "no" for an answer. *(Pause)*

Mary, if it worked for me it is going to work for you. It is really great and it's happening this afternoon. What do you mean, this afternoon isn't good? This is far too important to wait. You've got to come. If anybody needs it, it is you. *(Pause)*

Oh, I didn't mean it like that. I simply meant that you must come. Mary. I'm sorry. Wait, don't hang up.
(Looks at the phone startled, hangs up, and moves counterclockwise until her back is to the congregation)

#2: *(Dials phone)* Mary, I have discovered the greatest thing. No, no, I won't tell you what it is. You have to just come. This is the most fantastic thing in the world. *(Pause)* Why? Because we are such good friends and because this is such a fantastic opportunity that I want to share it with you. *(Pause)* That's right, I do consider you one of my best friends. *(Pause)*

What do you mean? *(Pause)* Come on now, I call you when I don't have some scheme up my sleeve. *(Pause)* No, this is not a sales pitch. Well, maybe it might be construed to be something like that. *(Pause)*

OK, if that's the way you feel about it, see if I care. Goodbye. *(She hangs up and moves counterclockwise until her back is to the congregation)*

#3: *(Picks up phone and dials it)* Hello, Mary? *(Long pause)* Oh, my. *(Pause)* I understand. *(Pause)* You seem a little down. Two tough calls, huh? I feel bad. Is there anything I can do? *(Pause)* Need to get out, huh? *(Pause)* Do you have any suggestions? *(Pause)* Well, I was going to a meeting this afternoon at my church. Maybe you would like to go? *(Pause)* No, no, the dress is casual. Can I pick you up? All right, I'll be there at 1:30.

See you later. *(Pause)* Oh, and Mary, afterwards let's go have some coffee. I have a feeling that there's a lot more on your mind. Bye. *(She hangs up)*

Exit

The Other Side Of The Fence

Topic: Materialism, priorities, greed, shortness of life, treasures in heaven

Characters: Peter and Penelope Piggie

Scene: The Piggies' living room. They whine through the whole script. When they turn around the two are wearing little pig noses. (These can be found at costume shops and novelty stores)

Peter: *(He is miming the opening of drapes and has binoculars around his neck)* Penelope dear, is that you?

Penelope: Yes, dear, it is I, or is that me? Why are you by the window again? You're just torturing yourself.

Peter: I know, but the Joneses just got a new boat. Look at it. It must be a seventy-footer if it's an inch. Why can't my boat be that big?

Penelope: Honey, your little boat is plenty big enough. Why, the whole family can fit on it.

Peter: Yeah, but it isn't new like their boat is. I want a new boat. One that can go as fast as theirs. Oh, and look at his new wife. Wow, is she thin! She must work out every day. That miniskirt sure is short.

Penelope: *(Grabbing the binoculars)* Let me see this. Why that's disgusting, running around like that in broad daylight. How old is she? Twenty?

Peter: She is pretty young. Well, old Jonesie sure knows how to pick them.

Penelope: Honey, what kind of car is that? I want one too.

Peter: *(Grabbing the binoculars)* It can't be. That is the exact car that I wanted. That is unfair. Why do they have everything in life? Why can't we have some of that good stuff too? I think I'm having a financial insecurity attack.

Penelope: Me, too. When can you make all the money that he has? Why can't I go to the health club every day like she does? Where's my new car?

Peter: And my new boat? *(Turning to his wife and putting down the binoculars)* Penelope, dear. I can only say that life is unfair. We work hard, we have filled our house with TVs, games, luxuries, and more. Then these Joneses move in and they have everything we have and then everything we ever dreamed of.

Penelope: *(Pouting)* Little Penelope is so disappointed that you haven't provided me with all those things. I trusted you to meet all my needs and — and, well, you've failed me. I'm beginning to think that you have failed at everything that you promised. There is no security in this relationship. I think it's time to end the whole marriage. You can go find yourself one of those bimbos like Jones did and give her everything that you promised me.

Peter: Dear, this is unfair. I work day and night. We have things stored away in every closet. We have enough stuff to last us forever and I can't understand how you can say that I haven't met your every whim.

Penelope: *(Looking out the window with the binoculars again)* When I look at him, I see a man that has everything. I mean, just look at him now. The caterers are delivering a meal. Lobster, crab legs, caviar, and cases of expensive champagne. Look at the way he's laughing and that cute little wife of his in the miniskirt seems so happy, too. I want to be just like them. *(Pause)* Although I must admit I don't like their taste in company. Who is that guy dressed in black?

Peter: *(Taking binoculars from her)* Which one? You mean the guy with the hood on?

Penelope: Yeah, that's the one. What is he carrying? It looks like a big stick with a knife on it.

Peter: I've seen that before in one of those *Little House on the Prairie* episodes. I think it's a reaper.

Penelope: That's grim.

A Handful Of Dandelions

Topic: Mother's Day, motherhood, joy of children

Characters: One woman

Props: Bouquet of dandelions

Scene: A house, no scenery needed

Mother: (*She is holding a bunch of dandelions in her hands*) All through high school, I couldn't wait until prom night when I would get a corsage of beautiful flowers. They smelled so sweet. I still have some of those things pressed away in *Webster's Unabridged Dictionary.* Filed under the letter of the boy who took me.

I guess I'm a little silly about it all. I think it's because I love flowers. When Joe and I got married, we had flowers everywhere in the church and each table at the reception had fresh cut flowers. I really like flowers and have come to know the name of just about every one.

Joe, my husband, thinks I'm part bee. But he understands. Every anniversary, I get a long stem rose for each year we're married. The fiftieth is going to break him. I think he's started a savings account just for the flowers on that day.

Flowers are just so beautiful and so meaningful. Each bouquet says more and more about love and care. Have you ever noticed how delicate each little petal is? Or if you look inside, you see the pistil and stamen and the little pollen waiting to be taken on the legs of some buzzing honeybee to another flower, so more flowers can be born into this world. They are beautiful things that make everything they touch lovely.

This afternoon, Joe is taking me to get my flats of flowers for the gardens. Now, that's where I'll spend most of my afternoons and weekends. Out there digging, planting, fertilizing, and watering. It is so peaceful. So quiet. I get a lot of time with God when

I'm down on my knees digging. It's good time. It's needed time. It's our time, God's and mine.

Yes, I love flowers. And I used to think that the more expensive the flower, the more valuable it was. I said "used to." That was until today. Joey, Jr. walked in just a few minutes ago, his face beaming. His smile showed off all those little baby teeth and he was so proud, so excited to give me something. I stooped down so I could look in those bright little eyes — if only they could have that innocence forever. It was then that he thrust into my face a lovely bouquet of flowers. Not expensive ones. Not rare ones. But ones that come with the hurricane force of a child's love. He gave me these — dandelions.

One time they were weeds that I wanted out of my beautifully manicured yard. Now, they've become the most beautiful flower a mother can see or hold or touch or smell. I used to like roses. Now, a handful of dandelions is my favorite.

Oh, I'm sorry, I've really gone on here. I've got to go anyway because dandelions are a multi-purpose flower. Did you know that if you rub them under your chin and it turns yellow, it reveals the answer to that age-old question, "Do you like butter?" Joey wants to find out if he likes butter. I just think he wants to be tickled. So I better pull out the old tickle fingers (*waves fingers in the air*) and get to work.

(*Turns to leave, pauses, and turns back*) Yeah, a mother's work is never done, but the high salary makes up for it. *She holds up the flowers*) Joey, honey. (*Calling to son*)

Exit

How Do You Spell Stress?

Topic: Tranquillity, serenity, marriage, work, children, bills, troubles

Characters: 2 males, 2 females, 1 either

Scene: Freeze frames. Each character performs lines then freezes in place

Male 1: How do I spell stress? Just like everybody else: I spell it J-O-B. I go into work and my boss is on my case right away. He wants this report and that meeting has to be attended. It's insane in that office. They've been cutting back and several of the people under me were let go. The company calls it downsizing for a leaner, meaner machine. About the only thing that's getting meaner is me. They downsize and the business gets bigger and bigger. I'm supposed to handle more, with less, in less time and for less money.

My territory now covers six states instead of three. I've doubled the customers and the quality keeps dropping. I can't tell you how many times I've had to say, "Your order is on the loading dock," when I know the company is having trouble producing it.

Did I mention the commute? What a ride! Me — I spell stress, J-O-B.

Male or Female: How do I spell stress? M-O-N-E-Y. I write the bills until there isn't any money left. Nothing at all. I'm wearing shoes that have been resoled twice, and now the resoled resole has a hole in it. They're OK as long as it doesn't rain. And then there's the kids' dental bills. I wish we had dental insurance. These bills are starting to get out of hand with all the braces and fillings. Now I discovered that the roof is leaking and needs "major repairs," according to the estimator. Do I have to go on?

We just don't make enough money. There is always more month than there is money. Sometimes I think about moving to Wisconsin and starting a little cheese store. You know, simplify my life a little. How do I spell stress? M-O-N-E-Y.

Female 1: How do I spell stress? Oh, that's an easy one. K-I-D-S. Everyday there's a new battle, a new scrape, a new fear, or a new boy that doesn't like me anymore. These kids don't know what problems are. But they will. Because they'll have kids, one day. I hope they have lots, just to punish them. And I hope their kids are just like they are. I'm planning on writing a book called *Men Are From Mars and Women Are From Venus and Kids Are From Hell.* Don't get me wrong. I love my kids. Dearly, in fact. But it is stressful around my house all the time.

And he is no help with the children at all. My husband, I mean. You would think that he would lift a finger around here but he doesn't. He says work is "sooooo hard" now that the company has downsized and he needs his rest. Sure.

Oh, yeah, and you should see what it's like in this house around Christmas. I won't begin to tell you about the list of toys and clothes they have and want and if they don't get them — they'll "just die." No doubt about it, I spell stress, K-I-D-S.

Male and Female Together: How do I spell stress?

Him: W-I-F-E.

Her: H-I-M.

Together: When I get home in the evening there …

Her: He is.

Him: She is.

Together: Acting like their day is the worst day in the history of employment. Granted their job is filled with stress but so is mine. When I come home …

73

Her: He …

Him: She …

Together: Expects *me* to cook dinner. I'm flat on my back with a headache and they want dinner because they're "too tired" to make it. What about me? And then the weekend hits and all I want to do is relax and take a break, put up my feet, sleep-in a little and they start in again with …

Him *(mocking her voice)*: When are you going to cut the grass?

Her *(mocking his voice)*: When are you going to clean the house?

Him *(still mocking)*: Let's go shopping.

Her *(still mocking)*: Let's go fishing.

Together: It's enough to drive you crazy. *(To each other)* By the way, my mother's coming to stay with us for a while. *(Both look shocked)*

(To congregation)
Him: I spell it W-I-F-E.

Her: I spell it H-I-M.

Exit

Topical Index

Encouragement — **The Invitation**
Ethics — **Behind My Back**
Ethics — **The Mask**
Evangelism — **The Invitation**
Evangelism — **The Mission**
Evangelism — **Pass The Buck**
Evangelism programs — **The Mission**
Evangelism training — **The Mission**

F
Faithful living — **1-900-MIDLIFE**
Food for spiritual health — **McChurch**
Fortitude — **Just A Mistake**
Friendship — **It's A Dog's Life**
Fulfillment through the fruit of the spirit — **Fruit Or Twinkies?**

G
Giving — **Behind My Back**
Greed — **The Other Side Of The Fence**
Growth — **McChurch**

H
Hard times — **The Answering Machine**
Head of church — **Born Leader**

I
Inner-city — **Here I Am, Lord; Send Someone Else!**
Introduction to the life of Abraham — **1-900-MIDLIFE**
Inviting neighbors to church — **Is It Really Worth It?**
Inviting others — **The Invitation**

J
Joy of children — **A Handful Of Dandelions**

L
Leadership — **Behind My Back**
Leadership — **Born Leader**

Lying — **Behind My Back**
Lying — **The Mask**

M

Marriage — **How Do You Spell Stress?**
Marriage — **Saturday Night At The Fights**
Marriage battles — **Saturday Night At The Fights**
Materialism — **The Other Side Of The Fence**
Midlife crisis — **1-900-MIDLIFE**
Ministry teams — **Born Leader**
Missions — **Here I Am, Lord; Send Someone Else!**
Mother's Day — **A Handful Of Dandelions**
Motherhood — **A Handful Of Dandelions**

O

Obstacles — **Because It Is There**
Organization — **Get With The Program**

P

Potential — **Get With The Program**
Prayer — **The Fool On The Hill**
Prayer — **The Mission**
Preparation — **Because It Is There**
Priorities — **The Other Side Of The Fence**

R

Relationship — **It's A Dog's Life**
Relationships — **Saturday Night At The Fights**
Reputation — **Behind My Back**
Responsibility — **It's A Dog's Life**
Responsibility of knowing Christ — **Pass The Buck**

S

Salvation — **Everybody Plugs Into Something**
Salvation — **Pass The Buck**
Seeking — **The Fool On The Hill**

Self-esteem — **Just A Mistake**
Serenity — **The Answering Machine**
Serenity — **How Do You Spell Stress?**
Servanthood — **Born Leader**
Services — **Behind My Back**
Shortness of life — **The Other Side Of The Fence**
Sincerity — **The Mask**
Slander — **The Mask**
Soulwinning — **The Mission**
Spiritual power — **The Fool On The Hill**
Stress — **The Answering Machine**
Summer Missions — **Here I Am, Lord, Send Somebody Else!**

T
Temptation — **Pass The Buck**
Testimony — **Behind My Back**
Tranquillity — **How Do You Spell Stress?**
Treasures in heaven — **The Other Side Of The Fence**
Trials — **Because It Is There**
Troubles — **The Answering Machine**
Troubles — **Because It Is There**
Troubles — **How Do You Spell Stress?**
Truth — **Behind My Back**
Truthfulness — **The Mask**

U
Unselfishness — **Born Leader**

V
Vision — **Just A Mistake**

W
Wisdom — **The Fool On The Hill**
Work — **How Do You Spell Stress?**